MALI

MALI

KIM NAYLOR

ACKNOWLEDGEMENTS

The Author and Publishers are grateful to the following organizations and individuals for permission to reproduce copyright illustrations in this book:

Mary Evans Picture Library; Ian Griffiths; Hutchison Photo Library; Jeremy Hartley/Oxfam; Popperfoto Ltd.

Other illustrations, including the cover and title page, are the copyright of the author.

Published by Chelsea House Publishers

Printed and bound in Hong Kong

First printing

ISBN 1–55546–181–6

Chelsea House Publishers

Harold Steinberg, Chairman & Publisher
Susan Lusk, Vice President
A Division of Chelsea House Educational Communications, Inc.

133 Christopher Street, New York, NY 10014

345 Whitney Avenue, New Haven, CT 05510

5014 West Chester Pike, Edgemont, PA 19028

Contents

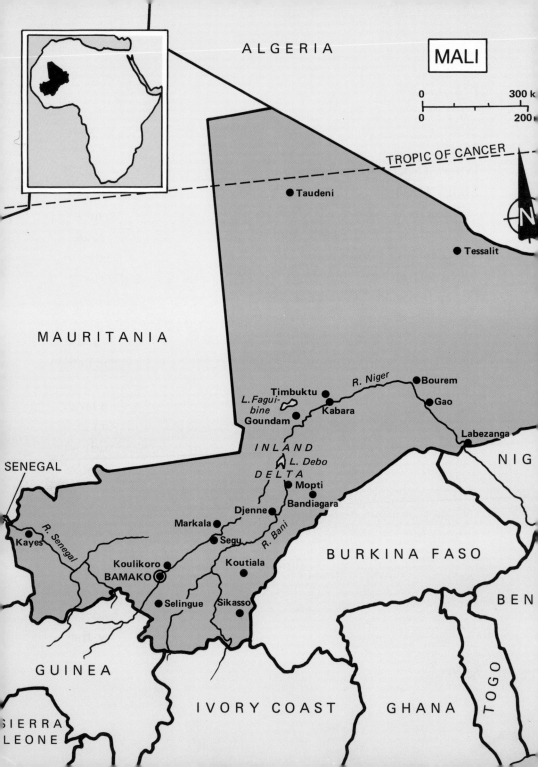

Where Desert Meets Forest

Mali is a landlocked country in West Africa. It is bordered by Algeria to the north, Niger to the east, Burkina Faso (formerly the state of Upper Volta), Ivory Coast and Guinea to the south, and Senegal and Mauritania to the west. It lies almost entirely within the tropics (the area between the Tropic of Capricorn south of the Equator and the Tropic of Cancer to the north), in a region where the dry Sahara merges into the wetter tropical vegetation of West Africa. For the most part Mali is a flat country and, with the exception of a few hilly outcrops, the land lies between 200 and 350 metres (650 and 1,150 feet).

All of Mali can be classified as hot and dry. But this is a large country—the second largest in West Africa (after Niger) and almost twice the size of Texas or ten times that of England. As it bridges the desert and the tropical forest, there is a range of different climates and vegetations within its borders.

There are two main seasons in West Africa and they are dominated by the southwesterly monsoon winds and the northeasterly trade winds. These winds play a particularly important role in determining the character of Mali's climate and hence its vegetation.

The northeasterlies blow down from the Sahara between November and June. Between November and January they bring a relatively cool dry wind known as the *alize;* from January onwards, however, the hot dry unpleasant *harmattan* wind blows and fills the sky with dust. Temperatures rise progressively, and are at their highest between April and June.

The southwesterlies blow from the Gulf of Guinea and bring the rains in June. Powerful winds and violent thunderstorms herald both the beginning and the end of the rainy season. The rains are heaviest during July and August when they fall in short showers every few days; the temperatures are then a little lower, but the atmosphere is humid. By November the rainy season is over throughout the country and the northeasterlies start to blow again.

The northeasterlies dominate the north of the country. Here the dry season is long and lasts for most of the year. Temperatures are high and they are at their highest in May when they average about 35 degrees Celsius (95 degrees Fahrenheit)—though they can reach 53 degrees Celsius (127 degrees Fahrenheit) in some places. The rainfall—if there is any—is minimal and sporadic and averages well under 20 centimetres (8 inches) per annum, falling in July and August. The impact of the winds diminishes as they blow towards the coast and their effect in the south of Mali is not as great as in the north.

The southwesterlies dominate the south of Mali. Here the rainy season can last for up to five months. Temperatures are still high, and they average about 31 degrees Celsius (88 degrees Fahrenheit). The rainfall is certainly more plentiful than in the

Scrub vegetation in the hot, dry north of Mali

north and ranges from 60 centimetres (25 inches) in the area around Mopti to 140 centimetres (55 inches) per annum in the far south.

Naturally, this climate determines the type of vegetation found in Mali. The very hot, dry north of Mali—the vast empty area to the north of a line across the country which cuts through Timbuktu—is sandy desert and forms the southern part of the Sahara. The severe climate here does not allow much growth. Indeed, the furthest north crops can grow without the assistance of irrigation is latitude 15°N; this is known as the "Crop Line". Most of the precious rain evaporates. However, a small amount seeps into the soil and does, in some areas, allow the growth of a little herbaceous plant, known locally as *acheb*, which

The Sahel, the dry savannah zone which lies between the northern desert and the southern tropical forests

provides grazing for animals. There are also a few small oases where dates are cultivated.

Progressing southwards, the desert gradually gives way to a dry savannah area, with outcrops of grasses, bushes and trees. This in turn gives way to tropical vegetation in the very south of the country. The transitional savannah zone, lying between the desert and tropical forests, is known as the Sahel. It runs along the southern limits of the Sahara right across the width of Africa from the Atlantic Ocean to the Red Sea. The Sahel runs through the middle of Mali and is about 300 kilometres (200 miles) deep from north to south. The climate is still hot and dry, but it is not as harsh as in the desert regions. The southwesterlies are more effective here than in the north of Mali;

the rainfall ranges from 20 centimetres (8 inches) per annum in the north of the Sahel to 60 centimetres (25 inches) in the south. Even so, this is not a lot of rain; as a result the natural vegetation is sparse and consists of hardy grasses and trees and bushes such as baobabs and acacias.

The Sahel merges into the tropical vegetation zone just south of Mopti. The southwesterlies bring sufficient rain to give growth to forests with trees such as the silk cotton tree, the two ball nitta tree, the shea butter tree, dum palm and other vegetation.

Flowing through Mali is the River Niger, one of the world's great waterways. Its importance to Malians cannot be over-stressed.

The great River Niger, Africa's third longest river

The River Niger has its source in the Fouta Djalon Highlands of Guinea, near the eastern border of Sierra Leone. From here, only 240 kilometres (150 miles) from the Atlantic Ocean, it pushes northeast through the Sahel to the southern limits of the Sahara. Then it turns east and finally southeast to the Gulf of Guinea, where it discharges its waters into the ocean through the numerous streams of the Niger Delta. Thus the course of the River Niger forms a huge arc. From source to mouth it measures 4,160 kilometres (2,600 miles), which makes it Africa's third longest river after the Nile and the Zaire (formerly known as the Congo).

Millions of years ago, the Upper Niger was linked to the River Senegal. A dry period followed which resulted in a barrier of sand forming between the two rivers. Consequently the Upper Niger changed its course and flowed northeast into Lake Arouane, the southern part of which used to extend to the area now covered by Mali's Inland Delta region. Then the climate became wetter. To the east, fast-flowing streams cut their paths southwards from the Adrar des Iforas and Air regions of the Sahara (roughly where the present borders of Mali, Niger and Algeria meet) and joined up as one big river near the present-day town of Gao. From here the Lower Niger, as it is known, headed south towards the sea.

During the same wet period, Lake Arouane overflowed and a river channelled its way east and met up with the Lower Niger at Gao. Thus the link between the Upper and Lower Nigers was created and the course of the River Niger as we know it

12

was formed. Another dry period followed: the original headwaters of the Lower Niger dried up, as did Lake Arouane. Lakes like Lake Faguibine and Lake Debo and the Inland Delta (the region from Segu to just east of Timbuktu) are relics of this once huge Saharan lake.

Nowadays the annual rains cause the River Niger to flood the Inland Delta and the area affected by this inundation is the size of England and Wales, or the size of the state of Georgia in the USA.

Most of the 1,500-kilometre (938-mile) stretch of the River Niger which flows through Mali passes through the dry, fairly barren Sahel savannah belt. Here, in particular, it serves as a lifeline to hundreds of thousands of people: the river provides water for consumption and for the irrigation of fields along the banks; it is also an important source of fish.

However, the River Niger is more than a lifeline. It was, and still is, a vital means of communication, rather like a highway passing through the Sahel. This is very significant because once, hundreds of years ago, the lands now encompassed by the borders of present-day Mali were involved in a thriving trade with the countries north of the Sahara; and the River Niger provided an essential transport link between the great market towns of the Sahel.

Mali's History

THE GREAT SAHELIAN KINGDOMS

Some two thousand years ago, the Sahara was, as it is today, a vast waterless expanse bordered to the north by what is now known as the Maghreb. (This is the strip of land in northwestern Africa between the Sahara and the Mediterranean Sea—in other words, present-day Morocco, Algeria and Tunisia). The southern border of the Sahara is formed by the Sahel.

From about the fourth century A.D., the Berbers—the indigenous "white" race of people from the Maghreb—were crossing the desert on camels. Gradually trade developed between them and the people of the Sahel. As a response to this trade, the Sahel settlements began organizing themselves into kingdoms.

The rise, wealth, stability and eventual downfall of these kingdoms depended to a great extent on the trade which passed through their lands. The Arabs who conquered the Maghreb desperately wanted gold and they soon realized that the Bilad al Sudan—"The Land of the Blacks", as they called the countries south of the Sahara—had it in abundant supply. The gold was in the tropical forests, just south of the Sahel, and this dry savannah belt became a buffer zone between the Arabs in the north and the Blacks in the gold-producing areas of the south.

14

Traders from the Bilad al Sudan—known as *dyulas*—would barter for gold in the south and take it to their market towns, where they would exchange it mainly for salt with the Arab merchants.

Three of Africa's greatest kingdoms rose and fell successively—Ghana (dating from the sixth to the thirteenth century and not to be confused with the present state of Ghana), Mali (thirteenth to fifteenth century) and Songhai (fifteenth to late sixteenth century). These kingdoms, and in particular Mali and Songhai, covered much of the land now lying within the borders of the modern state of Mali.

Rumours of magnificent wealth deep in the interior of the Dark Continent—as Africa was then called—filtered through to Europe. One such tale was of the famous Malian king, Mansa Musa, who embarked on an extremely lavish pilgrimage to Mecca in 1324. His entourage included five hundred slaves and one hundred camels laden with gold. Along the way he took every opportunity to show off his opulence. While he was in Cairo he was so generous with his gifts of gold that its price fell in the markets. It was not only Mansa Musa's fame which spread far; it is estimated that two-thirds of the gold for the European and Arabian mints early in the fourteenth century passed through the Sahel.

Market towns such as Gao, Djenne and the legendary Timbuktu also gained great reputations. Leo Africanus, a celebrated sixteenth-century Arab traveller, had the following to say about Timbuktu:

The rich king of Timbuktu has many plates and sceptres of gold, some whereof weigh 1300 pounds and he keeps a magnificent and well furnished court....He hath always three thousand horsemen, and a great number of footmen that shoot poisoned arrows, attending him. Here are great stores of doctors, judges, priests and other learned men, that are beautifully maintained at the king's cost and charges. And thither are brought divers manuscripts or written books out of Barbary, which are sold for more money than merchandise.

In the latter part of the sixteenth century, a European merchant in Morocco witnessed the arrival of a desert caravan,

16

almost certainly from Timbuktu, and mentioned that it had "such infinite treasure as I never heard of. It appears that they have more gold than any other part of the world besides".

The desert crossing was extremely arduous. The routes followed by the trading caravans were no more than a series of oases five to ten days' distance from each other. Although the journey was made during the mild season, the heat was still intense and there was no guarantee of finding provisions along the way. A merchant would only make a single crossing in any one year; each trip would be tempting death and five trans-Saharan voyages were considered enough for any man in his lifetime.

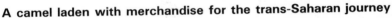

A camel laden with merchandise for the trans-Saharan journey

Sijilmasa, south of Fez, was Morocco's major caravan terminus until it declined in the seventeenth century. The journey from Sijilmasa to the salt mines of Taghaza in the very north of Mali, took three to four weeks and from there it was another two months to the southern terminus of Timbuktu. The most treacherous part of the journey was south of Taghaza. The only water between these salt mines and Walata, which is in southern Mauritania near the Mali border, was at Bir al Ksaib, ten days out of Taghaza. The caravans could not carry enough water from here to Walata, so guides were sent ahead of the main party to collect water from Walata; they would then double back, about four days' journey, to meet the caravan. This task was made particularly difficult because of the shifting sand dunes in this region and failure to meet led to certain death for the main party. In 1805, a complete caravan of two thousand men and eighteen hundred camels perished because they ran out of supplies while on their way to Timbuktu.

Some of the best guides were blind; by feeling and smelling the sand they managed to find their way across the desert.

Products brought by the traders from the north included glass beads, silver and copper goods, simple manufactured products from Europe and salt. By far the most important of these was salt which was collected at the Taghaza mines and carried in block form on camels to the markets of the Sahel.

The Sahel had a very limited quantity of salt at Dendi (around the Benin-Niger-Nigeria border) and the transporting of small quantities of sea salt from the Senegal coast did not prove viable.

A Tuareg, a member of a nomadic tribe. In the past the Tuaregs played an important part in transporting merchandise across the Sahara. Even today some of them still carry slabs of salt on their camels from Taudeni to Timbuktu

The traditional alternative was the saline residue obtained by sifting ash or scraping millet stalks.

Salt was in such demand that the merchants would often exchange it for an equal weight in gold. In the eighteenth century Mungo Park, the Scottish explorer, stressed its value:

In the interior countries, the greatest of luxuries is salt. It would appear strange to a European to see a child suck a piece of rock-salt as if it were sugar. This, however, I have frequently seen; although, in the inland parts, the poorer class of inhabitants are so rarely indulged with this precious article, that to say a man eats salt with his victuals is the same as saying he is a rich man. I have myself

19

suffered great inconvenience from the scarcity of this article. The long use of vegetable food creates so painful a longing for salt, that no words can sufficiently describe it.

Taghaza, the important mine between the eleventh and sixteenth centuries, was a desolate place. Ibn Battuta, an Arab traveller in the fourteenth century, wrote that it was: "......an unattractive village, with the curious feature that its houses and mosques are built of salt, roofed with camel skins. There are no trees there, nothing but sand. In the sand is the salt mine." The black slaves who cut blocks of salt four metres (thirteen feet) underground throughout the year were the only inhabitants. These men were expected to live for about two years under these conditions. The mine depended completely on passing caravans for its food: dates from the north and millet and sorghum from the south. If a caravan failed to arrive then the workers perished.

The salt was cut into slabs of around one metre (three feet) by thirty centimetres (one foot); those which were streaked with red and grey veins in a similar way to marble commanded a lower price than the pure white blocks. Merchants in Timbuktu would buy some five hundred slabs at a time and sell them for twice the price at Djenne.

In the second half of the sixteenth century, the Moroccans, under Sultan Ahmed el Mansur, invaded the Sahel and Taghaza closed down for good. New and bigger deposits were found at Taudeni, 700 kilometres (438 miles) north of Timbuktu. Conditions were equally appalling, and as recently as 1910 fifty-six workers died because the supply caravans failed to arrive. Today the Taudeni mines are still in operation and they are, apparently, worked by convicts.

The merchandise arriving in the Maghreb from south of the Sahara included slaves, gold, hides, kola nuts (a popular edible nut grown in the wetter regions of West Africa), ostrich feathers, leather goods and dyed cloth. Gold was the most important export item passing along the trading network which existed in the lands of present-day Mali.

Timbuktu is located near the northern bank of the River Niger at the point where the great river is closest to the markets of Morocco on the other side of the Sahara. It was also very significant that Timbuktu was linked by the River Niger to Gao—which had important trading caravan routes to Tunisia and Egypt—and to Djenne, on the River Bani 400 kilometres (250 miles) to its south. Djenne is an island for part of the year and during the floods it is only accessible by water. It, like Timbuktu and Gao, was essentially a trading centre for merchants who brought goods from the north or south. Pirogues, the traditional type of canoe, provided the transport for salt from Timbuktu to Djenne and for gold travelling in the opposite direction.

The Sahelian merchants from the time of the kingdom of Ghana had a peculiar way of trading with the Blacks from the gold-producing forests to the south. A special class of merchants evolved known as *dyulas*. From Djenne, for example, *dyulas* would enlist as many as two hundred slaves to carry blocks of

21

Pirogues, the traditional type of canoe, still used today just as they were in the long-gone days of the great Sahelian kingdoms

salt to the outposts of the gold-producing regions such as the Akan Forests and Kong, in the modern states of Ghana and Ivory Coast respectively. The salt and any other goods would be left at a predetermined spot and the *dyulas* would then retreat. The forest-dwellers would then appear and put quantities of gold next to each item before returning to the forest. If the *dyulas* were satisfied with the amount, they would collect it, leave their goods and the transaction would be finished; if not they waited until the locals offered more gold. This went on until an agreement was reached. This method of exchanging was known as "Silent Trading".

Over the centuries the *dyulas* built up a complex network of trade routes deep into the forest belt. Because of their trustworthiness the gold-collectors would deal only with them; the *dyulas* cleverly kept their sources a secret. It was largely because foreigners were prevented from learning the whereabouts of the gold that the west Sahelian states prospered for such a long time.

Through its contact with Arabs, the Sahel region began to adopt many Arab customs. The most important of these was the religion of Islam. Over the centuries large numbers of peoples became Muslims (the name given to the followers of Islam) and the *dyula* merchants were influential in spreading the faith throughout the Sahel and into the tropical forest regions. Today, Islam is the official religion in Mali and some sixty-five per cent of the population are classified as Muslims.

In Europe stories of unimaginable riches in the Dark Continent excited all those who heard them, but it was not until the end of the eighteenth century that the first explorers were sent to Africa. Amongst the earliest adventurers to penetrate deep into the western Sahel were Mungo Park, Gordon Laing, René Caillié and Heinrich Barth. The main objectives of these men were to locate and chart the course of the River Niger and to search out the remote Timbuktu, a dazzling eldorado somewhere in the centre of Africa.

After hazardous, courageous journeys these men reached their goals, but there was little trace of the magnificence they had hoped to find. René Caillié, a Frenchman who, in 1828, became

23

the first European to reach Timbuktu and to return to Europe, was not impressed with what he saw:"....the sight before me did not answer my expectations. I had formed a totally different idea of the grandeur and wealth of Timbuktu" and he concluded, "in a word, everything had a dull appearance". Had Europe been deceived by false stories of splendour? Was the alleged magnificence of Timbuktu just a myth? No, not really; a golden era had existed and flourished, but it had come to an end late in the sixteenth century.

The kingdom of Songhai ruled much of the western Sahel in the sixteenth century. It, like the earlier kingdoms of Ghana and Mali, thrived because it served as a middleman between the trans-Saharan merchants and the gold-mining communities in the southern tropical forest areas. Towards the end of the sixteenth century the Moroccans, under Sultan Ahmed el Mansur, wanted to cut out the Songhai link and have direct access to the gold mines. This resulted in the Battle of Tondibi near Gao in 1591, where the Songhai were heavily defeated and consequently their kingdom collapsed.

The Moroccans took control of Timbuktu, Djenne and Gao. For a while they managed to export a reasonable amount of gold across the desert—enough anyway for el Mansur to be nicknamed *el Dzehebi*, "the Golden".

But the invasion was expensive in both lives and money and, largely because the Moroccans never really gained control of the mines, the amount of gold crossing the Sahara did not justify these losses. Thus, early in the seventeenth century, the Sultans of Morocco lost interest in the Bilad al Sudan. They had destroyed the highly organized and successful Songhai state system and left behind little more than anarchy. Caravans continued to cross the desert, but the golden era of Saharan trade was now in decline. By the time the first European explorers reached this part of Africa, almost two hundred years later, it was a thing of the past.

COLONIALISM AND INDEPENDENCE

After Songhai the lands of Mali divided into smaller kingdoms and, though some of these were powerful between the seventeenth and twentieth centuries, they never really managed to equal the greatness of the old kingdoms of Ghana, Mali and Songhai.

In the second half of the 1800s a dramatic new era—the era of European colonialism—started to gather momentum in Africa. The major European powers of the time carved up the continent between themselves and it was France which gained possession of much of the Sahara and the Sahel belt of West Africa.

The French had long established trading posts along the coast of Senegal, Mali's western neighbour. Over the years the French had become increasingly influential in Senegal and in the latter part of the nineteenth century they were eager to push further east and expand their territories. This they achieved after defeating the local kingdoms.

In 1883, the French reached and occupied the small town of

Bamako on the River Niger. Five years later they built a railway between Kayes, on the River Senegal, and Bamako.

By the early years of the twentieth century the French had colonized vast areas of West Africa and nearly all the western Sahel region lay within their control. What is now Mali became known as the French Sudan. Over the following years it was, from time to time, merged administratively with what are now Senegal, parts of Mauritania, Niger and Burkina Faso, all of which are former French colonies.

The Africans resented French colonial rule. They demanded independence. Slowly, the French allowed their African subjects a greater say in their own affairs and finally, on 22nd September 1960, the former colony of French Sudan became a fully independent state. It was renamed Mali, after the historic mediaeval kingdom of Mali. Modibo Keita, a leading figure in the fight for independence, became the new nation's first president.

Under Modibo Keita, Mali adopted strong socialist policies for its economy and politics and there were great plans to develop the country. However, many of the projects, most of which were state-run, were unsuccessful and the economy suffered. In 1968 Keita was overthrown by members of the armed forces led by Moussa Traore and he remained in detention until his death in 1977. Traore has faced opposition from sections of the population, though his most worrying problem is the drought which has periodically struck Mali ever since he has been in power. Traditionally Mali is friendly with both the USA and

Modibo Keita, the first president of independent Mali

the USSR and is on good terms with the other West African countries. However, there has been an ongoing dispute with Burkina Faso since the early 1950s—and this has, on occasions, erupted into military confrontation—over claims to border territories.

The Peoples of Mali

Mali covers a total area of 1,240,695 square kilometres (478,695 square miles) and has a population of over six million inhabitants, which means that its population density is six people per square kilometre (fourteen people per square mile). At face value this statistic is misleading because the people of Mali are not evenly distributed around the country. Where people live normally depends on the geography of the region. In other words, people will usually live in the areas where the climate and the vegetation are most favourable.

The lands of Mali not only cover several geographical zones, they have in addition been a meeting-point where the peoples of North Africa came into contact with the tribes south of the Sahara. So Mali is also like a cultural transitional zone where Arabs and Berbers mixed with Blacks.

The distribution of Mali's different ethnic groups follows a definite pattern. The population in the north of the country is dominated by people whose ancestors originally came from North Africa. Their influence diminishes further south in the Sahel belt, where the people are a physical and cultural mixture of North African and black. In the south of Mali, the vast majority of the people are black and they have been the least influenced by North Africa over the centuries.

28

Nearly sixty per cent of the land area of Mali is covered by desert. In this huge harsh northern region, the population density averages only 0.5 persons per square kilometre (0.75 persons per square mile). The far north is characterized by rolling sand dunes and stony desert. There are a few settlements—such as Taudeni and Tessalit—and small numbers of nomadic Tuaregs and Moors who eke out a very basic existence near the all too rare water holes. But besides these the very north of Mali is uninhabited.

The desert gradually starts to merge with semi-desert in the region to the north of Timbuktu. This is still an inhospitable terrain and the population remains very low. However groups of nomadic Tuaregs and Moors live here, roaming the vast empty, sandy expanses with their herds in search of patches of acheb and other pastures. In the dry season, from November to June, there is not enough vegetation to support the resilient nomads' requirements and so they migrate south into the Sahel and onto the banks of the River Niger, where they know they can graze their animals. Here they remain until the start of the rains when they return north to their homelands on the southern edges of the Sahara. This migratory pattern is known as transhumance. The nomads endure many hardships in a difficult environment.

The Tuaregs are sometimes referred to as the "Men of the Veil" because the men wrap a veil or headcloth—known as a *taguelmoust*—around their forehead, mouth and nose. They claim to originate from a group of Berbers who migrated from Libya

29

A Tuareg man wearing the *taguelmoust* (traditional veil)

to their present homelands from around the seventh century A.D.

The state borders of Mali, which were drawn by the French in 1947, indiscriminately cut through many tribal homelands. So, for example, the Mali-Niger boundary may pass through a tribe's territory, leaving half its lands and people in Mali, while the other half are in Niger. This is the case with the Tuaregs who, today, are scattered over extensive desert areas in Mali, Algeria, Libya and Niger. They are believed to number some 650,000 in total, though estimates vary widely.

Tuaregs live close to nature. Their camels, donkeys, goats and in some regions sheep and cattle, provide them with their meat, milk, wool, hides and also transport. The camel, in particular, is invaluable to the desert dweller. This beast of burden is able to carry a load of 225 kilogrammes (500 pounds), 40 kilometres (25 miles) a day without drinking water for three days. In emergencies man can kill the camel, drink the water from its stomach and eat its meat. If it were not for the camel, man would not have been able to cross the Sahara in the way that he has done for almost two thousand years; and the flourishing trans-Saharan trade and the magnificent kingdoms

A Tuareg woman with her colourful jewellery

of Ghana, Songhai and Mali would never have existed. The Tuareg owes his nomadic lifestyle to the hardiness of his camels and he has a tremendous love and respect for these noble animals of the desert.

In the past the Tuaregs played a part in transporting merchandise across the Sahara. Even today, some of them still carry slabs of salt on camel back from the salt mines at Taudeni to Timbuktu 700 kilometres (438 miles) to its south.

As nomads, the Tuaregs are constantly on the move. The tents in which they live are traditionally made from the wool of their animals. Their basic diet is milk and dates; meat is only eaten on special occasions. Dates, which are collected from the oases, are often called the "food of the desert" because they are extremely nutritious and do not easily go bad in the hot climate.

Women, children and the men not involved in nomadic activities remain at a base camp which is usually by an oasis. Here they may cultivate date groves and millet and vegetables in small patches of field.

The Tuaregs have a rigid class hierarchy and the "white" Tuaregs, who claim Berber origins, are at the top. In the past these "white" Tuaregs kept black slaves whom they bought at market towns like Timbuktu. Today the descendants of these slaves are known as *Iklan*. They form an important community in Tuareg society and they have certain occupations—which are regarded as lowly jobs—they are blacksmiths, cultivators at the oases and servants in the nomads' camps.

The Tuaregs have their own language, Tamacheck, which is related to the old Berber language, but as they have contact with other people—such as the Songhai, Peul and Moors—most are able to speak more than one tongue.

Moors occupy parts of the northwestern desert regions of Mali, but they are normally associated with Mauritania where they account for the majority of the population. The Moors are of Berber-Arab descent—though over the centuries there has been some interbreeding with Blacks—and the way in which they are constantly on the move with their goats, sheep, camels and cattle in search of new grazing pastures has many similarities to the Tuaregs' way of life.

South of Timbuktu is the heart of the Sahel. Most of this dry savannah belt is still too barren to support a sizable settled population. However, the great River Niger flows through the Sahel and along its banks and those of its tributaries are towns, villages, numerous homesteads and small farms. Various tribes inhabit the Sahel. The Tuaregs roam the dry eastern region along the Mali-Niger border. To their west, along the River Niger, are the Songhai.

The Songhai are descendants of the great Songhai kingdom of the western Sahel. The Sorke, a community of fishermen, were originally the dominant tribe amongst the Songhai peoples. Local legend relates how the Sorke had a large river beast with a golden nose ring and from time to time this beast would impose its will on the other Songhai, most of whom were farmers, and extort huge taxes from them. Finally a traveller passing the area

A village on the banks of the River Niger

was so outraged by this injustice that he killed the beast with a harpoon. The Songhai farmers were overwhelmingly grateful and they elected him king, and he, Za Alieman, became the founder of the Za dynasty. This was the first of three Songhai dynasties, although it was under the two later dynasties, between the second half of the fifteenth century and the end of the sixteenth century, that the Songhais ruled most of the western Sahel and, indeed, a fair proportion of West Africa.

Today the Songhais number about 300,000. They live in mudbrick houses in the bend of the River Niger with their main centre at Gao, their traditional capital. They are mainly black and they speak Sonaikine, their own language. Most Songhai are subsistence farmers who cultivate small plots of land, producing just enough food for themselves and their families.

34

The Sorke, however, continue to fish the waters of the River Niger.

Still in the Sahel belt, but to the west of the Songhai homeland, live the Peul. The Peul have spread all around West Africa and they are known by different names—for example: Fula, Fulbe, Bororo or Fulani—in different regions. The Peul are tall, thin and relatively light-skinned, and these distinct features led many people to believe that they were related to the Ethiopians.

A Songhai woman talking to two herdsmen in the Sahel

However, experts can trace the Peul language, Fulfulde, back to the very western part of the Sahel and they now think that this is their original home and that their looks are a result of mixed Caucasoid-Negro (White and Black) ancestry.

Traditionally the Peul, who number about 550,000 in Mali, wander in nomadic or semi-nomadic fashion in search of pasture for their cattle. These animals are of paramount importance as they provide milk, butter, cheese and blood—the main foods in the Peuls' diet. Goats are also kept for meat. The dairy products and hides can be exchanged for arable produce in the markets.

A Peul man who has cattle has status and prestige, and he, like the nomads in the north, scorns the settled farmers because he thinks that their lifestyle is easy and unmanly. Even so, in recent years, largely due to the drought, an increasing number of Peuls have settled down to cultivate the fields.

The Peuls' territory includes the Inland Delta of the River Niger. They share this region with the Bozo, who are related to the Soninke, descendants of the ancient kingdom of Ghana, who live in western Mali. The Bozo, numbering some 20,000, are concentrated in small communities living in mud huts along the banks of the River Niger and the other rivers and lakes in the Inland Delta. They, along with the Somono (another group of peoples living on the banks of the middle Niger) and Sorke, are Mali's main fishermen. The boats they use are traditional wooden canoes which have been used on the River Niger from time immemorial.

A Peul woman wearing huge traditional-style earrings

The Sahel belt of western Mali runs along the southern border of Mauritania and to the border with Senegal. This is the land of the Soninke—also known as the Sarakole—who are the descendants of the early kingdom of Ghana which flourished in this region between the sixth and thirteenth centuries. Since the French colonial era, many Soninke have migrated from their homelands. Some joined the French army or merchant navy and the male members of numerous families moved to commercial centres all around Central and Western Africa where they have a reputation as shrewd merchants and businessmen. Indeed, between twenty and seventy per cent of the working

Cattle at a waterhole in the Sahel

male populations of Soninke villages are absent, leaving the women, old men, children and hired workers to look after their fields. Some two-thirds of France's black African migrant work-force are Soninke from Mali, Mauritania and Senegal. The black Soninke people interbred over time with the Moors who are their northern neighbours. On the Senegal border to their south are communities of Kassonke and Tukolor peoples, but their most important southern neighbours are the Manding, with whom they are linguistically related.

Most of southern Mali is inhabited by the Manding, whose presence extends from the Gambia in the west to Burkina Faso

38

in the east and from the desert fringes in Mali in the north to the forests of the Ivory Coast in the south.

Mandings are Blacks who trace their origin back to the hills on the borders of Mali and Guinea and to the great mediaeval kingdom of Mali, which evolved from this region and controlled much of the western Sahel after the fall of the kingdom of Ghana and the rise of the kingdom of Songhai. They have their own language and the two largest groups of Manding-speaking people are the Malinke and the Bambara, who occupy most of southwest Mali.

Most Mandings are farmers. They are, however, famous for their itinerant bards or musicians—known as *dyelis*. *Dyelis* travel extensively around West Africa playing traditional instruments such as the *kora*, a twenty-one stringed lute-harp, which is unique to their culture. Every seven years, *dyelis* from all over West Africa congregate at the small town of Kangaba, which is in the heart of Manding territory on the banks of the River Niger just upstream of Bamako. Another special class of people from the Manding group are the *dyulas*, who have played an important role as merchants trading throughout West Africa for many centuries.

The Manding are the largest ethnic group in Mali and the Bambara, who number 1,665,000, are the largest Manding tribe. Not only do the Bambara account for a large percentage of the population, they also dominate the government and administrative posts.

The Dogons are an interesting group of people who are

39

cultivators living in the area between Mopti and the border with Burkina Faso. They are probably related to the Manding, as it is believed they migrated to their present homelands from southwest Mali in the fifteenth century to avoid being converted to Islam. The Dogons, numbering 250,000, are very independent people and they have shunned outside influences in order to preserve their unique way of life.

The heart of Dogon country is the Bandiagara Escarpment. Many villages cling dramatically and picturesquely to the side of the almost sheer 500 to 600 metre (1,665 to 2,000 feet) high cliffs. The original reason for living here was as protection against hostile tribes, but after the French had colonized the region earlier this century, some of the villagers moved down and built their mudbrick thatched-roofed homes on the sandy savannah plains. So nowadays one section of the village is perched on the face of the cliff, while the rest of it is on the flat ground immediately below.

The Dogons' culture is closely related to their complex mythology. Nearly every aspect of Dogon life is symbolic of something and has a parallel in mythology. For example, their wooden statues relate to mythological characters, while in their spectacular masked dances they enact mythological events. Even their villages on the plains are laid out in the crude shape of a man; each building represents a part of the body and is associated with Dogon myths.

Farming the lands in the tropical zone just to the south of the Dogon and the the east of the Manding are the Bobo, the

**Dogon mudbrick houses
with thatched roofs**

Minianke and the Senoufe. These three tribes are better known and are represented in larger numbers across the border in Burkina Faso and the Ivory Coast.

Sandwiched between the desert and the tropical forests, Mali has a range of climates and vegetations. Mali also has a variety of different ethnic groups because it is situated at a point where the Arabs and Berbers of North Africa merge with Blacks of the lands south of the Sahara.

So there is a pattern: in the north the hot, dry climate allows

Traditional Dogon paintings. The Dogons' culture is closely related to their complex mythology

the growth of very little vegetation. The population is very small and the people here, who are predominantly of Arab-Berber origins, lead a nomadic life with their herds.

Conditions improve to the south in the Sahel, but they are still harsh. The population is denser than in the north—especially in the relatively fertile region of the Inland Delta—but most people live on a subsistence level as pastoralists or small-scale farmers. The inhabitants of the Sahel are a mixture of Arab-Berber and Black.

In the far south of Mali, most people are black. The majority of Mali's population live in the southern regions of the country, because the climate, vegetation and other physical conditions are at their most favourable here.

The most obvious difference in the lifestyles of these groups is between, on the one hand, the nomadic peoples from the deserts of the north and, on the other hand, the settled peoples of the Sahel and south Mali. Large low tents are the homes of the nomads in the north, whereas in the rest of the country the majority of people live in traditional-style mud buildings.

Although mud buildings vary in style and architecture in the different regions of Mali, they do have certain similarities. The huts typically have four walls—rather than being of circular design—and the roofs are either flat and made of mud or conical in shape and made of thatched grass; the windows are small and without glass so as to limit the amount of sun, heat and dust which can enter the building. The interior is usually simple—comprising one or two rooms—and tends to be dark and cool. The earthen floor is swept daily to prevent the dust from settling.

In the old towns, such as Timbuktu, the mudbrick houses are sometimes more elaborate and may indeed be constructed in a terraced fashion and have more than one storey. From the outside, many of the traditional buildings in Timbuktu appear very ordinary—bare walls, often showing signs of disrepair, and small windows—although the doors, in many cases, are old and elaborately designed and made of heavy wood which was imported in the past from the south. But outward appearances can be deceptive, for within some of the grander houses there are several large rooms and a courtyard. In earlier centuries, wealthy merchants preferred not to reveal their prosperity for fear of falling prey to the marauding tribes which periodically harassed the inhabitants of Timbuktu.

Today in towns, and to a much lesser extent in the villages, the traditional mud architecture is being joined or replaced by buildings made of factory-manufactured breeze blocks and roofed with corrugated iron. In Bamako, modern western-style buildings are becoming increasingly common.

While dates and milk form the basis of the desert nomads' traditional diet, millet—and to a lesser extent sorghum and rice—are the staple food for the Malians of the Sahel and the south. Fresh, dried or smoked fish are commonly eaten in the riverside regions. Goat, sheep, chicken and less frequently beef are also eaten—although meat is a relative luxury amongst the poorer people.

Markets are held all the time throughout the country. They

Baking bread in Timbuktu

Going to market

have many overall similarities wherever they are, although each area does have its own particular characteristics.

Dogon markets, for example, tend to get going around midday. Throughout the morning, men with laden donkeys and crocodile-files of women with baskets stacked high on their heads trickle into the market area and take their positions. The market attracts people from a wide area around. It is not an affluent market nor is there an abundance of goods, but transactions take place and the scene is lively, happy and colourful.

Typically the market is made up of rows of squat, wooden-

45

framed shelters covered with millet stalks. Men and women sit under these shelters with their merchandise: the delicious small Dogon onions, peanuts, millet, chillis, rice, fruits, spices, dried fish are all neatly displayed in small piles. The local travelling salesman, who moves from one market to the next, has a stall with plastic trinkets, torches, batteries, rubber shoes and the ever-popular "Kung Fu" or "Bob Marley Lives" T-shirts.

In the morning, a cow and sheep are slaughtered and throughout the day grilled meat is available to order. The atmosphere is mildly festive—maybe this is because of the *kojo*. The Dogon—who have a strong non-Islamic heritage and therefore do not consider it wrong to drink alcohol—brew a potent millet beer called *kojo* (known by various names and made elsewhere in Africa). Brewed by women, it is put, still fizzy and fermenting, into large earthenware pots. The drinking area is usually in the shade of a large baobab or mango tree, around which men will cluster and joke and catch up on the week's news over a few calabashes of thirst-quenching *kojo*.

Styles of clothing vary from tribe to tribe. The desert nomads wrap a length of cloth around their heads as protection against the sun and dust. They also wear the traditional *jellabahs,* which are loose gowns reaching down to the ankles and are cool and practical in the hot dusty desert. Indeed, *jellabahs* are worn throughout the country.

Further to the south, men usually wear a local style of shirt and trousers or shorts. In the villages, women commonly wrap a length of material, known as a *pagne*, around their bodies.

46

Drinking *kojo* (a potent locally-brewed millet beer) at a Dogon market

However, western-style clothing is becoming increasingly popular. A shirt, tie and smart trousers or even sometimes a full suit are worn by businessmen in Bamako. Women wear dresses and youngsters often wear shorts or jeans and T-shirts.

The official language in Mali is French though Bambara is the most commonly spoken tongue—especially in the southeast, which is the homeland of the Bambara people. Many of the tribes have their own languages or dialects which they speak in their own districts. Arabic is also spoken, particularly in the north of the country and within Islamic religious circles.

47

Today Islam is the official religion in Mali and some seventy per cent of the population are classified as Muslims. According to the teachings of Islam, God revealed divine truth to man in order to bring him back to a righteous way of life. These truths were revealed through a prophet; Adam, Noah, Abraham, Moses and Jesus were all prophets, but the greatest of all, according to Muslims, was Muhammad. Born in A.D. 570, Muhammad grew up to preach against the existing beliefs in his home town of Mecca, in present-day Saudi Arabia. Later he was forced to flee to Medina and it is this flight (the *Hejira*) in A.D. 622, that marks the first year in the Muslim calendar.

God's truths, the principles of Islam, were revealed to Muhammad by the archangel Gabriel and are documented in the Quran—the Muslim equivalent of the Bible. There are five "Pillars of Islam" which are of paramount importance to Muslims. These are the *shahada*, or testimony that there is no God but Allah and that Muhammad is His prophet; the *hajj*, or pilgrimage to the Kaaba (the black stone in Mecca that symbolizes the centre of the earth and universe) which should be undertaken by all Muslims at least once in their lifetime; the abstention from food, drink and worldly pleasures from daybreak to nightfall during Ramadan (the ninth month in the Islamic calendar); the giving of *zakat* (alms) to the poor—usually a small percentage of one's income; the *salat* (prayers), which are announced by the *muezzin* (an official attached to the mosque) five times a day—just before dawn, at midday, mid-afternoon, sunset and after dark. The prayer ritual of standing, kneeling
48

A Muslim festival. Some seventy per cent of Malians are Muslims, and Islam is the official religion of their country

and touching the ground with the forehead can be performed anywhere, as long as the worshipper faces Mecca.

The non-Muslims in Mali tend to adhere to their traditional beliefs in animism (spirit worship) and they are found mainly in the south and west of the country. There is also a small percentage of Christians.

A River Journey

Tourism is a small but valuable source of income for Mali. An interesting expedition for visitors is the boat journey along the River Niger through the historic and fascinating lands of the western Sahel.

The service operates during the high-water season—approximately August to December—and takes six days to cover the 1,308 kilometres (818 miles) from Koulikoro, Bamako's river port, to Gao, the downstream boat terminal.

The restful steamer journey is punctuated by a dozen or so

The steamer which operates on the River Niger between Koulikoro and Gao during the high-water season

ports of call and one of the first of these is Segu. In July 1796 Mungo Park first saw the River Niger from the west bank opposite Segu and so became the first white man to set eyes on the river. Park followed the Niger downstream and he was moved enough by one particular spot near the town of Sansanding to write: "At sunset we arrived at Modiboo, a delightful village on the banks of the Niger, commanding a view of the river for many miles...The small green islands...and the majestic breadth of the river...render the situation one of the most enchanting in the world".

Just upstream from Sansanding is the Markala Dam. Completed in 1947, the dam raised the level of the river by an average of four metres (thirteen feet). Boats pass through the 7-kilometre (4-mile) canal which runs parallel to the river. The area to the north of here along the Canal du Sahel (west of the Inland Delta) is the heart of an important agricultural project.

Mopti, 504 kilometres (315 miles) from Koulikoro, is the capital of the Inland Delta region. With little justification, Mopti, which is situated on three small islands at the confluence of the rivers Niger and Bani, has been dubbed the "Venice of Mali and West Africa". Comparisons aside, Mopti has its own charm. Though it has no real architectural beauty other than its marvellous spiky, mudbrick mosque, Mopti is a lively, busy market town centred around a small horseshoe-shaped harbour where the wooden canoes load and unload their merchandise.

Djenne, 85 kilometres (53 miles) southwest of Mopti, established significant trade links along the River Niger with

The port and market at Mopti

Timbuktu and developed as an important market. Europeans trading on the West African shores must have heard about Djenne's fabulous gold market from the black merchants (*dyulas*) of the interior. In an attempt to pronounce the African Djenne, they named the Guinea coast—where they were involved in bartering for gold—and subsequently the English "guinea" coin, after the city. In the seventeenth century Djenne's golden era began to wane, though it continued to be an important centre—particularly for Islamic studies.

Situated on the River Bani, Djenne is virtually an island for most of the year. Formerly this was to the city's advantage as it provided a water route to Timbuktu as well as a natural defence. But the trends of trade have changed and today Djenne stands isolated. Not linked to the outside world by proper roads, it has missed its opportunity to develop. Untarnished by modernization, Djenne is one of the most fascinating places to visit in West Africa.

In 1828, René Caillié became the first European to enter Djenne and his description of its market, the city, the houses and general character shows that it has changed remarkably little since then. Extracts from Caillié's nineteenth-century book *Travels through Central Africa to Timbuktu* give a reasonable picture of present-day Djenne.

The town of Djenne is full of bustle and animation; every day numerous caravans of merchants are arriving and departing with all kinds of useful products.

I paid a visit to the market; I was surprised at the number of people I saw there. It was well supplied with all the necessities of life, and is constantly crowded by a multitude of strangers and the inhabitants of the neighbouring villages, who attend it to sell their produce, and to purchase salt and other commodities.

There are several rows of dealers both male and female. Some erect little palisades of straw, to protect themselves from the excessive heat of the sun; over these they throw a length of cloth and thus form a small hut. Their goods are laid out in little baskets, placed on large round panniers.

In going round the market I observed some shops pretty well stocked with European commodities, which sell at a very high price....

There are also butchers in the market, who lay out their meat in much the same way as their brethren in Europe. They also thrust skewers through little pieces of meat, which they smoke dry and sell.

Great quantities of fish, fresh as well as dried, are brought to this market, in which are also to be had earthen pots, calabashes, mats and salt . . .

There are a great number of hawkers in the streets... They sell stuffs made in the country, cured provisions, colat (kola) nuts, honey, vegetable and animal butter, milk and firewood.

Large daily markets are now something of the past. However Caillié's description could well apply to the present weekly market which is held every Monday in front of the huge mudbrick mosque. The mosque itself, with its spiky spires, smoothly rendered walls and crude but elegant architecture, is one of the most spectacular and beautiful structures south of the Sahara.

The steamer travels down the River Niger from Mopti,

A lively market scene outside the mosque in Djenne

The channel linking Kabara (the port for Timbuktu) to the main stream of the River Niger. This channel was originally cut by Sunni Ali, the fifteenth-century Songhai king

entering the heart of the Inland Delta and Lake Debo, the Dark Lake, where boats crossing the waters from east to west lose sight of land for a whole day. The Niger divides into two main branches which join up again at Dire, the last stop before Kabara, the port for Timbuktu.

Kabara is connected to the main stream of the River Niger by a three-kilometre (two-mile) channel which was originally cut by Sunni Ali, the Songhai king, in the fifteenth century. Even during the high-water season, it is touch and go whether the canal is deep enough for the steamer: a flotilla of pirogues marks time, eagerly waiting and hoping, and if the steamer grinds to a halt then the piroguemen swarm around the boat. Passengers lower their baggage, goats, babies and finally themselves into these small traditional canoes which then provide, for a small payment, a shuttle service to Kabara. From here it is only nine kilometres (six miles) to Timbuktu.

Up until the beginning of the twentieth century, unprotected travellers on the Kabara to Timbuktu road were easy targets for local villains. Félix Dubois, a Frenchman who passed along this route at the end of the last century, commented that "the road half way between Kabara and Timbuktu bears a sinister reputation. The natives have given it the tragic name of *Our Oumaira* ('They hear not'), meaning that neither at Timbuktu nor Kabara can the cries of the victims be heard".

Around A.D. 1100 a tribe of nomadic Tuaregs started to graze its animals near the village of Hamtagal (just to the south of present-day Timbuktu). They discovered a small oasis here which they put under the surveillance of an old woman while they were away seeking new pastures. Some locals say that the old woman's name was Tomboutou, which means, apparently, "The mother with a large navel"—she must have had an umbilical hernia, a physical disorder which is still common in this part of the world. The settlement which grew up around this oasis was named after her and today there is a courtyard near the Sidi Yehia Mosque in Timbuktu which commemorates the spot where she handed out water to weary travellers.

Timbuktu was well positioned to play a significant role in the trans-Saharan trade. It is on the southern edge of the Sahara,

Donkeys in a dusty side-street in Timbuktu

near the most northern point of the River Niger. Canoes would travel from Djenne to Kabara and then by road to Timbuktu. Being away from the Niger's banks the town is little affected by the floods. At Timbuktu the cargo would be transferred to camels for the desert crossing north.

But after the fall of the Songhai kingdom Timbuktu suffered terribly; the legendary golden city degenerated hopelessly.

Today Timbuktu is in much the same state as it was when the first European explorers visited it in the nineteenth century. This grey, mudbrick town is sad, drab, dusty, devoid of trees and not particularly impressive. The three main mosques—Dyingereyber, Sankore and Sidi Yehia—are Timbuktu's greatest heritage, and the houses of Laing, Caillié and Barth still stand, commemorated by plaques. A smart French-run hotel

57

The house of Gordon Laing in Timbuktu

and a government guesthouse provide accommodation and food. There is a modern expensive, though poorly stocked, supermarket which looks out of place surrounded by scrappy mudbrick buildings and desert. Most of the streets are sand, there is electricity and running water, a post office and a bank, army and police camps, a few motor vehicles and a landing strip for small planes. But the character of Timbuktu remains much the same despite these modern additions.

From Kabara it is a further 400 kilometres (250 miles) to Gao. Much of the landscape along the banks of the "arc" of the River Niger is arid savannah or desert. Often the sand creeps right down to the water's edge, but sometimes the banks are rich with trees; irrigation schemes have developed large areas of flood plain for rice cultivation. During the high-water season, sections of the plain become vast sheets of water and at times it is difficult or impossible to determine the river's edge. A patch of solid land in the distance may give the impression of being the bank, but a closer look reveals another channel or expanse of water beyond it; much of the land through which the Niger flows becomes a lattice of interlacing channels and extensive marshland.

The flooding leaves small islands, quite a few of which support homesteads; horses and cattle have to wade out to their pastures and farmers paddle their canoes to their paddy fields. Attractive villages and homesteads are dotted along the banks of the Niger. The buildings are made from mudbrick and typically it is the unusual architecture of the mosque, with its stocky spires and protruding cross-beams, which catches the eye.

At the ports of call, a small crowd clusters around the quayside when the boat arrives. Many have something to sell: mats, hats, fruits, nuts, brochettes (pieces of meat on skewers), grilled fish, bread, tea, coffee. Friends and families are united. From the top deck of the steamer the passengers have a detached bird's-eye view of the colourful scene and gentle hubbub below.

Some 200 kilometres (124 miles) downstream of Kabara is Bamba. Because of its strategic position at a narrow point of the Niger, Bamba was important under the Songhais who depended on their control of the River Niger for their authority. Beyond is the Toysaye Gorge, the narrowest part of the Niger in the Sahel region, and then Bourem where the river suddenly turns from an easterly direction to a southeasterly course. Arabs

**Crossing the gangway
onto the River Niger
steamer at Bamba**

are believed to have first settled on the river around this area;
it is also the point closest to Egypt and legend has it that an
ancient Egyptian pharaoh once came here. On 4th January
1922, the Citroen expedition, led by Monsieur Citroen himself,
reached Bourem. These were the first cars to cross the Sahara.

From Bourem it is only another 95 kilometres (60 miles) to
Gao, a town built in the seventh century which grew to become
the capital of the great Songhai kingdom. Like Timbuktu, Gao
declined after the fall of the Songhai kingdom and, according
to Heinrich Barth, it was a "desolate abode of a small miserable
population" in the mid-nineteenth century.

Today Gao, much of which was rebuilt early this century,

is the downstream terminus for the River Niger steamboat and also the first stop in Mali for trans-Saharan travellers coming from Algeria.

It is a small, busy, bustling river port. The streets, set out in a grid pattern, are quite wide, but mostly unpaved, dusty and crowded; the buildings are ramshackle and of little architectural interest. (This is also true of the main mosque which was originally built by Mansa Musa in the fourteenth century.) As with so many Sahelian towns, however, Gao's charm lies in the atmosphere generated by everyday life.

So ends the river steamer journey (the Labezanga Rapids further downstream prevent continuation) through the lands which were once rich with gold and caught the imagination of the Arab and European world. From here the River Niger flows into the country of Niger and then Nigeria before discharging itself through a multitude of channels—which form a delta just west of Port Harcourt—into the Gulf of Guinea.

Dependence on Agriculture

The lands of Mali were once rich. Its kings were wealthy and its cities were splendid market towns for a flourishing trans-Saharan trade. However, the golden era when Mali prospered from trade is now in the distant past and today Mali is one of the poorest countries in the world.

Agriculture plays a central and very important role in all of West Africa's countries. Mali is certainly no exception—ninety per cent of the population are involved in agriculture, and ninety-nine per cent of its exports are agricultural products.

Nomads wander the northern part of the country in search of grazing for their animals; and settled farmers cultivate the soils of southern Mali. In the Sahel, cutting through the middle of the country, there are both nomads and cultivators. Fishermen are found all along the course of the River Niger and also the River Senegal in western Mali.

The majority of those involved in agriculture are subsistence farmers. This means that a man and his family produce only enough food to feed themselves; if there is a small surplus then it is exchanged in the local market.

The small-scale subsistence farmer often cultivates his lands through a method known as rotational bush fallowing. When the season is over, and the farmer has gathered his crop, he

A typical country scene. Malian farmers often use camels to plough their fields as well as to carry loads

will then leave his field lying fallow (unseeded) and move on to another field the following season. This process goes on year after year and the original field may lie fallow for several years. During this period the soil has a chance to build up its store of nutrients; hence when the farmer returns to the field it has regained its fertility and there is a chance of a healthy yield of crops.

The main crops grown by the small-scale farmers are millet and sorghum, which provide the basic diet for most Malians. Millet and sorghum are farmed extensively throughout the Sahel belt and are the most important food crops in this part of Africa.

They are hardy cereal crops able to grow in poor soils and to survive under hot, dry conditions. Both plants reach a height of between one and four metres (three and thirteen feet) and their grains have a high nutritional value. About one million tonnes of millet and sorghum are produced in Mali each year.

While millet and sorghum are grown essentially for home consumption, cotton and groundnuts are Mali's main ''cash crops''. They are sold abroad to earn money to buy commodities that Mali does not produce itself, such as oil and manufactured goods like cars and machinery.

Initially it was the European colonial powers who introduced the concept of cash crops, or commercial farming as it is sometimes known, into their colonies during the late nineteenth and early twentieth centuries. They needed lands where they could grow the crops which they were unable to cultivate at home

Sorghum. This hardy cereal is one of the main crops grown in Mali. It forms the basic diet for most Malians.

and these they would send back to their own people in Europe. For example, Britain developed sugar-cane plantations in its West Indian colonies and extensive tea farms in India and its East African colonies. These commodities were shipped to Britain either for home consumption or to sell to other European countries. Today cash crops, so often a legacy of a past colonial ruler, provide the backbone of the economy in many West African countries.

Today most of the cash crops are sold to the western world at a relatively low price. This is unfair because the manufactured goods, such as cars and machinery, that the western countries sell in return are usually very expensive. This is the reason why many developing countries such as Mali remain poor. Without money they cannot develop their own manufacturing industries, hence they will continue to be dependent on the western world for manufactured products.

Depending on one or two crops is like putting all one's eggs in one basket. For example, the world prices of the crop may slump and consequently the revenue earned from the exports will be low. Disease or drought can strike and destroy a large proportion of the nation's agriculture and, therefore, the livelihood of many of its people.

Though Mali is not as dependent on one single crop as some of its fellow West African countries—the Gambia, for example, relies on groundnuts for over ninety per cent of its foreign revenue—it is, however, totally reliant on agricultural produce for its export income. Cotton accounts for fifty-seven per cent of foreign earnings, groundnuts eighteen per cent, live animals fourteen per cent, and fish, cereals, fruit, vegetables and leather make up nearly all of the rest.

Mali's greatest, most horrific problem is drought, which constantly haunts the whole Sahel belt the width of Africa and strikes with devastating and tragic results every few years.

The terrible drought of 1972–74 caused the death of an estimated 100,000 people in the western Sahel region. Those worst effected in Mali were the Tuareg and Moor pastoral nomads. Probably the greatest casualty of the drought, however, was the livestock which was one of Mali's most important exports (the animals would be walked across the borders to neighbouring countries where they would be sold). Before 1972, Mali had an estimated six million head of cattle and fourteen million goats and sheep; some sources claim as many as eighty per cent of the herds perished. Crops and fish also suffered badly and overall food production dropped by thirty-seven per cent. Foreign aid was forthcoming and thousands of destitute, hungry families walked to the towns and centres where they received food and medicine. By July 1974 there were about 80,000 refugees in thirty camps in the Gao region alone.

With the death of their animals, the Tuaregs and Moors not only lost their source of livelihood, they also lost their dignity. There were sad, pathetic scenes of these proud, independent desert people squatting in cramped makeshift camps, faced only with the humiliating option of accepting charity from the aid organizations.

66

Children in a relief camp. International charity organizations have saved the lives of many people in the famine-stricken regions of Africa but the problem is unlikely to disappear completely

In 1975 the rains returned. However the effect of the drought on Mali's people, its agriculture and its economy had been catastrophic. The slow recovery was hindered by further disasters such as low rainfall, followed by freak flooding along the River Niger in 1978–79. This forced the government to import 60,000 tonnes of cereal crops and to announce in 1980 that there was a food deficit of 250,000 tonnes. The 1980–81 crop season was very poor and the World Food Programme donated wheat in order to prevent widescale starvation. But in

1982–83, the rainfall was sixty-five per cent below average and the Malians were once again faced with the terrible threat of drought. Crops failed and livestock died in much of the Sahel belt in 1984–85. The result was another major famine. The appalling plight of Africans from countries such as Ethiopia, Sudan, Chad, Niger, Burkina Faso and Mali was given a tremendous amount of publicity on television and in the newspapers all around the world.

Appeals aimed at the American and European public by charity organizations, such as Band Aid and US Aid, collected large sums of money for the famine-stricken regions. This money bought food, clothes, medicine and also tents for the camps and vehicles to transport all the goods. Though large numbers of lives were lost through starvation and disease, many were saved by charity.

The countries of the Sahel have a harsh and difficult environment. The people are at the mercy of the climate and they depend on the erratic annual rainfall to provide them with their food. Sadly the rains will continue to fail again and again and measures must be taken to combat drought and prevent another recurrence of terrible mass starvation.

Mali's Economy

Mali is a poor country and its economy depends on the success of its agricultural output. Mali will more than likely remain a poor country first because its agriculture, and hence its economy, can fail because of poor climatic conditions, and second because of the relatively low price paid for its crops by other countries around the world.

The average income of most Malians is very low. Some two million Malians, who want jobs with better money, have left their homes and now work abroad—usually in richer West African countries like Nigeria, Ghana, Liberia, Sierra Leone and, in particular, the Ivory Coast where they can earn a lot more money. There are about 400,000 migrant workers from Mali working in the Ivory Coast alone.

On the one hand, the exodus of workers abroad is advantageous because they send the money they earn back to their families in Mali and this is good for the country's economy. However, on the other hand, it is a disadvantage when able young people, especially skilled workers and professionals, go abroad and thus deprive their own country of their much-needed talents.

Even within Mali there is migration from the poorer parts of the country in the north to the richer southern region. Though

69

ninety per cent of the population are still rural dwellers, there is a definite trend towards the main towns.

The high birth rate, running at 2.5 per cent a year, and the drop in the infant mortality rate, thanks to improved medical facilities, has led to a large young population throughout the country. This can lead to pressures on the farming lands. For example, on his death a farmer will leave his plot of land to his sons. When they die they in turn will divide their plots between their sons. So at each generation these inherited plots of land get smaller and smaller. However, each son has to support his own family on the produce of his plot of land. If there is not enough food for everybody then he, or members of his family, may move to the towns to look for other jobs.

Indeed there has been quite a remarkable migration from the rural areas to Bamako, Mali's capital city. Bamako was a small old Manding market town on the River Niger in the southern part of Mali. In 1883 the French colonists made it their base for further penetration into the interior.

On independence, Bamako became the capital of the new state of Mali. Consequently it became the centre for politics, administration, commerce, industry and culture. Its population grew rapidly. In 1958 it had 76,000 inhabitants; in 1966 this figure had risen to 170,000 and ten years later it was 404,000. Today the population of ''greater Bamako''—that is the city itself and the villages within a 30-kilometre (20-mile) radius— is thought to be around 800,000.

It is estimated that fifty per cent of the present population is under the age of twenty. If the level of migration to the city and the population growth continue at a high rate, then Bamako will have to construct many new buildings to accommodate all these people.

At present, Bamako is surprisingly undeveloped and the visitor is not confronted by a skyline filled with cranes and buildings under construction. There are a handful of modern buildings (most notably international banks, a sports stadium and a couple of international class hotels). However, the view from the top of the Hôtel l'Amitié, Mali's only skyscraper, is of clusters of squat, reddish-brown, mudbrick houses on one side while on the other side flows the majestic River Niger

A view over Bamako from the top of the Hôtel l'Amitié

crossed by the Pont du Niger—the only bridging point (besides barrages) of the river in Mali.

Some of the migrant workers find accommodation on the outskirts of the city where they can rent small rooms cheaply. Others live in the villages and new settlements which have sprouted up around Bamako. Bamako does not have, at least not yet, the squalid, overcrowded shanty towns which are so common in overpopulated, rapidly expanding cities of the developing countries.

What kind of job can a migrant worker hope to find? As Bamako is a growing city, it needs labour to work on the construction of buildings and roads and also in any industries which may evolve. As the city grows, so does the demand for service industries and here there is a large variety of opportunities.

Today the bustling market area in the centre of Bamako is packed with small shops selling food, clothes, electrical goods, spare parts; there are also cafés, food stalls, bicycle and motorcycle repair shops; men wander around selling cigarettes, peanuts, snacks, soft drinks. There are banks, hotels, restaurants and a large market where people can buy their meat, fish, fruit and vegetables. Demand for these, and many other service industries, will increase as Bamako gets bigger.

Much of Bamako's supply of fresh fruit and vegetables comes from the market gardens in the surrounding lands—there are even small cultivated plots along the city waterfront. Growing food for the urban dwellers offers further job opportunities.

Small groups of craftsmen are found scattered around central Bamako. Most are from Manding country—the region to the west of Bamako—but there are others from elsewhere in Mali. Particularly common are the weavers, though at the Craftsmen's Market there are a range of artisans who work in wood, metal, clay, cloth. They usually sell their crafts to visitors and tourists.

In addition to the regular flow of migrant workers, there is the seasonal influx of the *barani*—seasonal workers—who arrive in Bamako looking for work between January and May when there is little for them to do on their fields in the rural areas. Though job opportunities are created in developing cities, the problem of more workers than jobs is extremely common in

The entrance to Bamako market

A view of small cultivated plots in the centre of Bamako

many cities around the world. It is a problem which now faces Bamako.

Bamako has a fortunate location in Mali. Being in the very south of the country it does not suffer the severe climate experienced by places further to the north and it is unlikely that it will be affected by the extreme horrors of drought and famine. It is also relatively well placed for Mali's involvement in foreign trade.

Being a landlocked country, Mali does not have its own seaports, so Dakar in Senegal and Abidjan in the Ivory Coast serve as its gateways to the outside world. Bamako's position on the River Niger gives it easy access to both these ports.

Nearly all Mali's overseas imports and exports pass through either Dakar or Abidjan. The Dakar–Bamako railway was started by the French because they wanted a transport link between the coast and the lands they had colonized in the interior of West Africa.

In 1888 the French completed the first leg of the railway between Kayes, on the River Senegal, and Bamako; this was later extended to Koulikoro, Bamako's port, which is just downstream of the Sotuba Rapids. Hence the navigable stretch of the River Niger between Koulikoro and Gao was now linked to a navigable point on the River Senegal, which flows through Senegal and into the Atlantic Ocean. So the French had created the link which provided a means of communication from the sea right into the heart of the western Sahel. Early in the

Bamako railway station. The first stretch of railway in Mali was built by the French in the 1880s. It linked Bamako to Kayes on the River Senegal

twentieth century, the railway line was continued from Kayes to Dakar. This made it possible to travel by train the whole way from Dakar on the Atlantic Coast to Koulikoro on the River Niger—a distance of 1,290 kilometres (806 miles).

The single-track railway passes through western Mali where there are some steep gradients and many small rivers and streams. Maintenance of the track is difficult and expensive and, though many improvements have been made over the years, the whole railway network and rolling stock is not really adequate for the volume of traffic.

Mali's railway system is run by the Régie des Chemins de Fer du Mali (RCFM) which transports 340,000 tonnes of merchandise and 600,000 passengers a year.

There is no through road between Bamako and Dakar and a fair proportion of Mali's overseas imports and exports travel by road, on the route via Sikasso between Bamako and Abidjan.

Bamako is Mali's trading hub. Imports arrive in Bamako from Dakar and Abidjan and from here they are distributed around the country. Exports, on the other hand, are brought from around the country to Bamako from where they are taken to Dakar or Abidjan.

Mali has about 13,000 kilometres (over 8,000 miles) of road of which only 1,700 kilometres (1,000 miles) are bituminized. 3,350 kilometres (over 2,000 miles) of roads are seasonal—this means that bad weather, usually resulting in flooding, prevents their use for part of the year.

The road network is at its best in Mali's most populous and

agriculturally richest southern region southeast of the River Niger. The most important route is the busy two-lane bitumen road from Bamako to Mopti via Segu (Mali's two main towns after Bamako, each with a population of around 60,000).

A 560-kilometre (350-mile) road is being planned from Mopti to Gao which will link with the road across the Sahara between Gao and Tamanrasset. Merchandise and people travel between Bamako and Mopti either by road or by barge on the river. Beyond Mopti the main means of transport at present is the River Niger.

Expensive imports, such as manufactured goods, machinery, fuel, food and other commodities cost Mali a lot of money. Indeed, Mali has a serious trade deficit. That means that the amount of money paid for imports is much more than the amount of money earned from exports.

Hopes for the Future

How can Mali reduce and eventually wipe out its trade deficit? Mali has the potential to feed itself and if this goal were achieved then there would be no need to buy from abroad the food which accounts for a large slice of the imports.

Mali is investing large sums of money in developing its agriculture. One of the oldest, most important development projects is controlled by the Office du Niger.

The proposal to irrigate and develop a dried-up area of the Inland Delta of the River Niger (which lies to the southeast of the existing Inland Delta) was put forward by Emile Bélime in 1925. The French wanted to develop cotton as a cash crop in Mali because they needed it for the French cotton industry. In addition they hoped to attract farmers to this region and away from the more populous, overcrowded neighbouring farming lands. By establishing commercial farming they planned to improve the overall standard of life and provide long-term economic security in western Sahel after the famine which had devastated this area in 1914.

In 1932, the Office du Niger was inaugurated and it announced ambitious targets: in fifty years, 960,000 hectares (2,400,000 acres) would be under cultivation. Of this, 510,000 hectares (1,275,000 acres) would be cotton and the remaining

78

Agriculture in the River Niger area. Large-scale irrigation schemes are the key to success in Mali today

450,000 hectares (1,125,000 acres) would be devoted to rice.

The water level of the River Niger was raised by building a dam at Markala; canals were constructed into the irrigation zones and many farmers, mainly from the Bambara and Peul tribes, moved here to farm the new plots of land.

Initially, however, there were problems. The nearest seaport was 1,500 kilometres (935 miles) away at Dakar and it proved expensive, laborious and time-consuming to bring the machinery and the other necessities all that distance from the coast. The French agricultural experts did not know enough about the local environment and, largely because the soil was not suitable, there were pests and the drainage was poor, their attempts to grow cotton in the region were not successful. Cotton was eventually abandoned, although the cultivation of rice has continued.

The Office du Niger did not meet its optimistic goals. By the late 1970s, a total of only 41,000 hectares (102,500 acres) were under cultivation and of these 39,500 hectares (1,000,000 acres) were given over to rice. Sugar-cane, which grows on the land not occupied by rice, has shown promising results.

Up until the late 1960s, sugar was almost exclusively grown in the traditional way on small family plots. Today there is now a sugar distillery and a sugar refinery with a capacity of 20,000 tonnes per annum; there are hopes that Mali will eventually become self-sufficient in sugar.

The development of rice production has become increasingly important in recent years. Large-scale irrigation schemes have made productive huge areas of land along the banks of the River Niger. Particularly significant are the farming projects centred around Timbuktu and Gao in the otherwise barren Sahel belt. The other main rice-growing centres are around Segu, Mopti and the Office du Niger region. A lot of money is being devoted to the expansion of rice cultivation; yields have improved dramatically, but as yet they do not match the level of home consumption. In 1979 Mali produced 279,000 tonnes of rice and it is hoped that by the year 2000 there will be an annual output of two million tonnes.

The River Niger is rich in fish and has one hundred and eighty different species of which the Nile perch—nicknamed "Le Capitain"—is the most famous. The fish have a migratory pattern which revolves around the flooding of the river. As a result the fishermen, who are mainly from the Bozo, Somono and Sorke tribes, traditionally lead a semi-nomadic life, following the fish along the course of the river. Almost ninety per cent of the catch is from the Inland Delta and lake regions, and Mopti is the main centre and market for fish. Most of the fish are dried, salted or smoked and in many villages along the banks there are small earth stoves where the process can be seen in action. Charcoal is burnt in the lower section of the stove and the fish are laid immediately above on a wire grill so as to receive the full effect of the smoke.

In recent years the fishing industry has become increasingly important to Mali and accounts for three per cent of the country's exports; most of these fish are sent to Ghana, Burkina Faso and the Ivory Coast. The government are keen to develop the fishing industry and, under *L'Opération Pêche,* they intend to provide sophisticated factories for the storage, treating and packaging of fish. 100,000 tonnes is the annual fish haul and about 200,000 people are involved in the industry from the catching to the final selling stage.

Although cotton failed in the Office du Niger region, it is now growing successfully in the very south of Mali. The area immediately southeast of Bamoko is the cotton heartland and is agriculturally and economically the richest part of the country. The main centres for cotton are Sikasso, Bougouni, Koutiala and also Bamako where there are cotton-processing factories. The government's economic plan in the 1970s was to expand the growth of cash crops for export, and cotton and groundnuts

Smoking fish

were their main products. In 1971 cotton accounted for thirty-three per cent of Mali's export revenue; in 1978 it was worth fifty-seven per cent and yielded some 135,000 tonnes.

Groundnuts, once Mali's top revenue earner, now rank second in the export ladder. Groundnuts are grown in an extensive area just north of Bamako, spreading in a belt from the Senegalese border to the region of Segu. Despite the fall from prominence, groundnuts are still important and there is hope for an increase in yields over the next decades.

Tea and tobacco are grown on a modest, though commercial, basis in the south of the country. They are unlikely to ever feature significantly in the exports but they do, however, contribute to the home market.

82

The Institut d'Economie Rurale (IER), a department in the Ministry of Rural Development, is in charge of agricultural progress. Its task is to help improve the agricultural output of the country by providing aid and education to the farmers.

While the many government and overseas organizations are concentrating their time and money on the development of agriculture for export, they must not forget the small-scale subsistence farmer who, after all, provides the vast majority of Malians with their staple diet of millet and sorghum.

Packing groundnuts, Mali's second largest export crop

Without initial financial assistance the farmer can easily be caught up in the "subsistence spiral". In other words, if a farmer has no money he cannot buy seeds, fertilizer—the average amount of fertilizer used in Mali is just one-tenth of the amount used in Africa as a whole—or good farming equipment. Hence his harvests will be poor; there may be sufficient food to feed his family, but he will not have enough crops to sell and therefore no surplus money to buy seeds, fertilizer or new equipment for the following year; and so the cycle continues.

With help from the IER, the farmer has the chance to improve the yield of his crops and he can sell the surplus in the market. With the money he earns, he can improve his farm and generally raise his and his family's standard of living.

The failure of the government to invest in the small-scale subsistence farmers has had some adverse effects on the economy. There is a familiar pattern throughout West Africa: attracted by the monetary gains of commercial farming, the subsistence farmer abandons his traditional crops (millet and sorghum in the case of Mali) and instead plants a cash crop—such as cotton—which he can later sell for a profit. As more land and manpower are devoted to cash crops, less attention is paid to the all-important staple foods. This means that there is not enough food grown at home to feed the population and hence the government has to spend its precious money on importing food.

There is another problem leading to the shortage of food. In the interest of the people living in the towns, the government has announced that farm produce cannot be sold for more than a certain amount of money in the markets. This law has had serious repercussions because farmers are now smuggling their crops, and also cattle, across the borders to countries like the Ivory Coast where they can sell them for four times the rate allowed by the Malian government.

Large-scale millet and sorghum farms are being created. Here they use modern machinery, fertilizers, pesticides—to prevent disease—and sophistocated farming techniques. At present such projects are in their infancy, but they promise to boost the output of these two very important crops. It is unlikely, however, that these large farms will ever take over completely from the small-scale farmer.

The grandest, most impressive and probably the most fruitful development scheme being undertaken at present is the Senegal River Valley Development. At the centre of the project is the Selingue Dam on the Sankorani River, 224 kilometres (140 miles) from Bamako in western Mali. The hydroelectricity produced here is for consumption in Bamako and also for industrial developments. Once fully completed the scheme will create a 430 square kilometre (165 square mile) lake which will yield a catch of 3,000 tonnes of fish a year and there will be scope to irrigate and farm 57,000 hectares (142,500 acres) of land between Selingue and Markala.

Ten thousand people will eventually lose their homes because of the construction of the new lake, but they will be resettled elsewhere in the region.

If the spectacular Senegal River Valley Development reaches its planned capacity, there will be a tremendous increase in agriculture in the lands between the River Niger and Senegal. This whole area is a potential "breadbasket" of West Africa.

Not only will the Senegal River Valley Development help Mali achieve its target of food self-sufficiency, it will—thanks to the amount of hydroelectricity generated—reduce its expensive oil imports which account for a substantial portion of the country's overseas spending bill. Oil products are costly enough in themselves, but in addition there is the high price to pay for their transport overland from the coast through either Senegal or the Ivory Coast to Mali.

Further hydroelectricity projects are under way and the developments in thermal and solar energy will contribute to Mali's energy requirements and hopefully lessen its dependence on oil imports even more.

The extent of Mali's own mineral wealth is not really known at present. Salt, the great trading commodity from north of the Sahel in the past, is still mined at Taudeni. At one time famous caravans, known as *azalis*, would trek with up to four thousand camels laden with salt from Taudeni to Timbuktu. Today Taudeni has an output of three thousand tonnes a year. Gold, the main item exchanged for salt in the mediaeval period by the people south of the Sahel, is now exploited in a modest way at Kalana in southwest Mali. There is an estimated reserve of 24 tonnes of gold and it is hoped that production will reach 400 kilogrammes (900 pounds) per annum.

About two thousand tonnes of phosphates are mined each year near Bourem. Bauxite and iron ore have been discovered in reasonable quantities in southern Mali, west of Bamako, and there are uranium deposits in the northwest of the country. Various companies, most notably Elf Aquitaine, have been prospecting for oil in recent years, but without success as yet. It is still early days for minerals in Mali and further exploration may reveal substantial resources.

However, one of the problems hampering the exploration is the difficulty of travelling around the country. North of Mopti, roads are either unreliable or non-existent. New roads, such as the one between Mopti and Gao, are being constructed but this vast northern area will remain undeveloped until communications are improved.

Industry—found almost exclusively in Bamako and the southern region—is on a small and modest scale. Most of the enterprises are state-owned and are limited to the processing of local products such as cotton, vegetables, tobacco, rice and fruit juice. There are also small assembly factories which put together bicycles and farm machinery and implements.

Manufactured goods account for a large proportion of Mali's annual imports and they will continue to do so until Mali makes substantial advances in its own industrial development.

In the long term, education will be a key to Mali's development and future prospects. In 1962 the government launched a programme to reshape the educational system which they had inherited from the French. They built new schools and less than twenty years later 350,600 children—boys and girls—were attending elementary classes, compared to 75,000 in 1962. The number of students attending further education has also increased substantially. Those wanting a university education must go abroad—usually elsewhere in Africa, to France or even to the United States or the Soviet Union—as Mali does not have a university of its own. However, there are small colleges which offer practical courses in agriculture and land-use, engineering and medicine.

Despite this drive to improve education, only thirty per cent of children go to school and only three per cent of the 20- to 24-year-old age group attend higher education colleges. This is partly because the population is expanding quickly and there are not enough schools to cater for the youngsters. Though education is vitally important, Mali cannot immediately afford to build all the schools it requires. The majority of schools are in the southern region.

Many parents, particularly in the rural areas, prefer their children to help in the fields rather than go to school. Some children are sent by their families to attend the traditional Quranic classes under the guidance of a *marabout*—an Islamic religious teacher. Here the child is taught the religious disciplines of the Islamic faith and must also learn by heart passages from the Quran, which is the Muslims' religious book.

French is usually regarded as the official language and is widely spoken by people throughout the country. However, each region and tribal group of people speak their own language and

88

A Quranic student waiting for alms

Bamana—the tongue of the Bambara peoples—is referred to by some as the national language and is used in political and government circles.

It is compulsory to learn French at school and schoolchildren are at least bi-lingual, being able to speak their own tribal or regional language, French and possibly Arabic.

Naturally education is directed towards the youth and very few adults have had the opportunity to go to school. Ninety per cent of Mali's adult population is illiterate. However, government programmes have been established around the

An immunization
programme at a rural
health clinic

country to provide farmers with practical information on how fertilizers, pesticides and basic technology can improve their agricultural yields.

The overall standard of health in Mali is still far from satisfactory, but it has improved in recent years. There are ten hospitals in Mali's main towns, and on average there is one doctor for every 75,750 people. However the greatest concentration of medical facilities are in Bamako and its environs where, for example, there are several hospitals and a ratio of one doctor for every 25,000 people.

Many diseases can be avoided by adopting simple hygiene measures. Drinking polluted water, for example, can cause

90

severe illness. Nowadays, tap and pumped water in towns and villages is often cleansed of impurities and is safe to drink.

Tropical diseases like bilharzia, trachoma, trypanosomia and malaria are still common in Mali, but medicines, simple health education and an improvement in hygiene have enhanced the overall quality of life. As a result, by 1978 the average life expectancy had increased to forty-two years compared with thirty-seven years in 1960. At the same time the death rate had decreased. For example, in 1960 forty-one children out of every thousand were expected to die between the ages of one and four; by 1978, this ratio was thirty-two deaths per thousand children. The improvement of the nation's health has led to the rapid increase in the growth of Mali's population.

Mali is developing slowly. However, a disproportionate amount of the development projects, services, money and attention is concentrated in Bamako and the southern part of the country. Most of the government officials are Mandings from either the Malinke or Bambara tribes and it is probably in their interest to encourage the development of their homelands in southern Mali. Fortunately there is now a gradual push towards decentralization. This means that greater efforts are being made to develop and provide opportunities and facilities in the regions all around the country.

Southern Mali will always remain the "centre" of the country, because it has the physical advantages of a favourable climate, the richest agricultural lands, the greatest concentration of natural resources so far discovered and the easiest access to the sea ports. But decentralization will benefit the whole country, not least because it will relieve the population pressure on the south by encouraging people to stay in their home regions, rather than going to places like Bamako to find work.

How can Mali, a poor country with a substantial trade deficit, afford to undertake expensive development programmes? Much of the money for Mali's many development programmes comes from financial grants received from abroad. France, the United States, the Soviet Union, China and Germany are the main donors. The Soviet Union, for example, built air-strips at Gao and Mopti and provides scholarships for Malians to study at colleges in the Soviet Union. China has been involved in some thirty projects since Mali's independence from France and is currently helping with the construction of dams. France still has ties with her former colony and, in addition to being an aid donor, it is also Mali's strongest trading partner buying over thirty per cent of its exports and providing forty per cent of its imports.

The International Development Agency (IDA) and the Africa Development Bank have made available considerable sums of money to Mali. This money has been spent on many projects, such as the construction of roads, the development of farm lands, education, health, the improvement of the railway system, the sinking of wells and the development of industry.

There are, however, drawbacks to accepting aid. Unfortunately the rich country usually outlines certain conditions when it provides money and assistance to a poorer, developing country. The rich donor country may say, for example, that it will only give help to the poorer country if it can have a military base in its territory, or if it can buy cash crops at a low price. If these demands are not met, then the aid will not be forthcoming.

Mali is dependent on the richer donor countries for development, though the conditions for accepting this help are not as unfavourable as in the cases of some developing countries.

Even so, greater independence from donor countries is desired and possibly lies in the success of organizations such as ECOWAS and CEAO. The Economic Community of West African States (ECOWAS) comprises all the West African countries, and the Economic Community of (Francophone) West Africa (CEAO) comprises Mali, Mauritania, Niger, Senegal, Burkina Faso and the Ivory Coast. The objective of each of these two organizations is to unite its member countries and encourage them to help each other with their development programmes, so that they will eventually become economically independent and no longer need the aid—with all its "strings attached"—of an outside donor country.

At present, Mali's prospects of becoming economically independent look like a distant hope, but one day this great historic country may prosper through trade as it did in the past.

Index

95